Making Decisions

Selina Li Bi

Reader Consultants

Brian Allman, M.A.
Classroom Teacher, West Virginia

Cynthia Donovan
Classroom Teacher, California

iCivics Consultants

Emma Humphries, Ph.D.
Chief Education Officer

Taylor Davis, M.T.
Director of Curriculum and Content

Natacha Scott, MAT
Director of Educator Engagement

Publishing Credits

Rachelle Cracchiolo, M.S.Ed., *Publisher*
Emily R. Smith, M.A.Ed., *VP of Content Development*
Véronique Bos, *Creative Director*
Dona Herweck Rice, *Senior Content Manager*
Dani Neiley, *Associate Editor*
Fabiola Sepulveda, *Series Designer*
Ana Sebastian, *Illustrator, pages 6–9*

Image Credits: All images from iStock and/or Shutterstock

Library of Congress Cataloging-in-Publication Data

Names: Bjorlie, Selina Libi, author.
Title: Making decisions / Selina Li Bi.
Description: Huntington Beach, CA : Teacher Created Materials, [2022] |
    Includes index. | Audience: Grades: 4-6 | Summary: "We make decisions
    every day. Some choices we make are easy and some are not. There are
    many things to consider when making a decision. It can be challenging,
    but you have the power to choose!"-- Provided by publisher.
Identifiers: LCCN 2021045455 (print) | LCCN 2021045456 (ebook) | ISBN
    9781087615387 (paperback) | ISBN 9781087628790 (epub)
Subjects: LCSH: Decision making--Juvenile literature.
Classification: LCC BF448 .B56 2022 (print) | LCC BF448 (ebook) | DDC
    153.8/3--dc23/eng/20211108
LC record available at https://lccn.loc.gov/2021045455
LC ebook record available at https://lccn.loc.gov/2021045456

TCM | Teacher Created Materials

5482 Argosy Avenue
Huntington Beach, CA 92649
www.tcmpub.com

ISBN 978-1-0876-1538-7

Table of Contents

Decisions, Decisions 4

 Jump into Fiction:
   Snowballs 6

Your Brain and Decisions 10

Steps to Decision-Making 12

Feelings 20

Making Good Choices 24

Responsible Decisions 28

Glossary 30

Index 31

Civics in Action 32

Decisions, Decisions

What should I eat for breakfast? What color socks should I wear? Which movie should I watch tonight? Decisions, decisions. Whether you are **aware** of it or not, you make many decisions each day.

So, what is a decision? It is a choice you make about something. There are usually two or more **options**. People can make most decisions on their own. But sometimes, they have to ask for help.

Everyone makes hundreds or even thousands of decisions every day. Some decisions are easy, such as which shoes to wear to school, or whether you want strawberry or vanilla ice cream. Some decisions are more difficult, such as who to sit by on the bus. And some decisions are really difficult. What if you see a classmate being bullied at school? What should you do?

As you get older, you'll have plenty of decisions to make. There will be different levels of **complexity**. Making responsible decisions can be challenging!

Jump into Fiction

Snowballs

At recess, Jamie swung on the swing, pumping her legs toward the sky. She searched the playground for her best friend, Teresa, but there was no sign of her anywhere—just the school's meanest bullies, Blade and Cooper, marching toward Jamie with snowballs in their hands. Jamie's legs grew heavy, and the swing swayed lower to the ground.

"Scramble, doofus! It's our turn," yelled Blade, as he stood by the swing set.

"Yeah, we have total dibs on the swings, so beat it," added Cooper.

Jamie's heart thumped against her chest. She hopped off the swing and started to walk away.

She felt someone grab her arm and yank her to the side. It was Teresa. She whispered, "You have every right to be on the swings, too."

Just then, Blade hurled a snowball toward Jamie, and it grazed the top of her head as she ducked.

"You need to stand up for yourself," said Teresa.

Jamie's mind swam in circles, making her dizzy.

She could stand up to them, but if Mrs. Shelby thought she was fighting, she'd be in major trouble. Another option would be ignoring Blade and Cooper, but then Teresa would call her a wimp.

Jamie wanted to do the right thing—ignore it—but those bullies didn't own the playground. She decided to make a snowball.

"Bawk…bawk…chicken," teased Blade. "I dare you to throw it!"

"They deserve it," said Teresa.

Jamie patted the snowball, but her stomach began twisting into knots. She threw the snowball to the ground and stomped on it.

"I changed my mind. It's not worth it! Let's get away from here," Jamie said.

Blade hurled another snowball at her, but this time it almost hit Mrs. Shelby's leg!

"What are you two doing? Both of you go inside now," Mrs. Shelby said, furrowing her brow.

Cooper dropped his snowball to the ground. Cooper and Blade trudged toward the school, shoulders slumped.

"It's a good thing you didn't throw the snowball!" said Teresa.

"I know," replied Jamie. "That was a close call."

Back to Nonfiction

Your Brain and Decisions

How do you make a decision? To make a decision, you must use your brain.

The part of the brain that helps you make choices is called the *prefrontal cortex*. It is located in the frontal **lobe** of your brain. This part of the brain helps bring together your thoughts and actions. It helps you solve problems. The prefrontal cortex is the last area of the brain to fully grow. It is still growing even in teenagers!

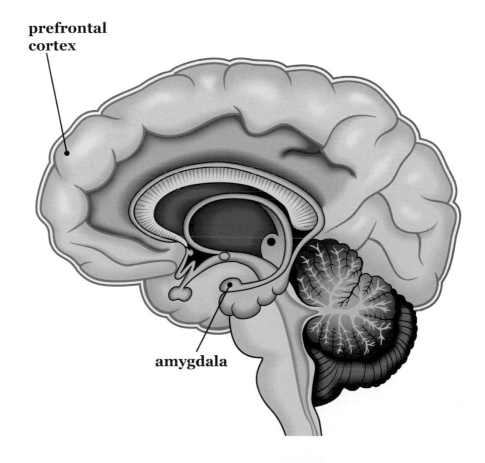

prefrontal cortex

amygdala

Fun Brain Fact

The human brain is made up of roughly 73–75% water. This is one of the reasons why it's so important to drink enough water! Not getting enough water can affect how the brain functions.

The **amygdala** is the part of the brain that deals with emotions. It is responsible for your **survival** skills. If you are in sudden danger, such as a fire, the amygdala prepares your body to act when there is danger. It **triggers** a fear response. Your heart races! Your palms sweat!

These parts of the brain influence your decisions. And the decisions you make are affected by many different things: your emotions, your **knowledge**, and your **experience** in the world.

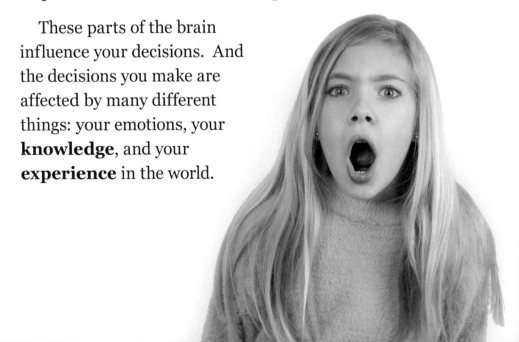

Steps to Decision-Making

The decision-making process involves six steps.

 Step 1 Identify Your Question

The first step is identifying your question. To make a healthy decision, you must first know exactly what you are trying to decide. So, the first step in the decision-making process is to clearly state the question or situation. Ask yourself, *What am I trying to figure out? Does this question need to be solved?* Perhaps you are trying to decide what to eat for breakfast. The question might be, *Should I eat a bowl of cereal or a bagel with cream cheese?*

Animals Make Decisions, Too

Studies have shown that animals have to make choices just like us. They have to decide when to eat and sleep. They must weigh the advantages and disadvantages of their choices just like we do!

Some decisions are more difficult and affect not only you but other people, too. What if you borrowed your friend's favorite jacket and you accidentally ripped it? The question might be, *Should I tell my friend I ripped their jacket?*

Think of a decision you had to make today. What would the question have been?

Gather Information

Once you have figured out what question you need to answer, you need to gather information. Find out everything you can about your situation. You might need to research using books or the internet. You may need to get information from other people.

You will also need to ask yourself, *What are my values?* A value is something people care about. It is their likes and dislikes. It is their needs and desires. To determine your values, you can think about what is most important to you right now. You can also think about what you can do without.

The internet can be a useful resource to help with many decisions, such as deciding where and when to see a movie.

Talking with other people can help you make decisions.

For example, you may have enough money for a new video game. Do you decide to buy it or not? You might decide to save your money or use it to buy something else instead. Knowing your values often helps you make decisions.

Sometimes, people have to make a choice to do what's right rather than what they want. For instance, you may decide to do homework instead of playing with friends.

Differences in Values

Values are very personal. Different people have different values. Sometimes, people's values are based on their cultural or religious beliefs. It can take time to develop values and determine what is important to you. Values tend to change over time, especially as people get older.

Brainstorm Options

Once you've defined your situation and gathered important information, then you can brainstorm ideas. Be creative. Be **flexible**. Make a list of all the possibilities!

Ask yourself, *What are all the possible options?* Try to think of as many options as you can. Ask a friend or an adult to help you brainstorm ideas. This can help give you a different point of view. It opens up other ideas you might not have thought of.

Group Decisions

Small groups can sometimes make better decisions than large groups. It's easier to decide on something when there are fewer people. Seven to nine people works best for a group decision!

Brainstorming can occur on paper, or you can talk through your ideas with other people.

You can also ask yourself, *How does this option affect me? How does this option affect others?*

Certain options might make you feel better than others. Cheating at a board game might help you win, but you might feel bad afterward. Maybe you want to go to the movies with your friends, but you promised your aunt that you would help her clean her house.

Our decisions often make an **impact** on our lives. Our decisions can affect other people, too.

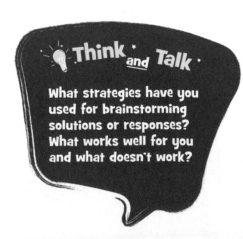

Think *and* Talk

What strategies have you used for brainstorming solutions or responses? What works well for you and what doesn't work?

Step 4 Consider the Consequences

After brainstorming ideas, you will want to think about each of your options. Choices people make often have consequences. Consequences are the results of those choices. Consequences can have different **outcomes**. Choosing to eat a candy bar right before dinner could have a negative outcome. You might not feel hungry at dinner time. Studying for a test instead of playing with your friends may have a positive outcome. You may earn a better grade.

Make a list of all your options. Think about the outcomes of each option. Ask yourself, *Which option seems the best? Which options have the best outcomes?*

Have you ever made a choice that resulted in something you were not happy with? Did you learn from that experience? You probably learned what not to do next time. Reflecting on past decisions and their outcomes can help you make new decisions.

Choosing how long to study can have different consequences.

Choosing between different food options can be tricky!

Feelings

Some options can make you sick inside or worried. Ask yourself, *What am I worried about? Will my decision hurt me or someone else?* How you feel might be a way to find out if you are making a good or a bad decision. Learn to trust your feelings and **emotions**.

Strong emotions can have a big impact on our decisions.

Emotions

Our emotions can be spread to other people like colds. We can "catch" good and bad feelings from others. If your friend is feeling down about something, you might start to feel sad just like them!

Your feelings can affect how quickly or slowly you make a decision. If you are angry, you might be in a hurry to make a quick decision. If you are afraid, you might take longer to make a decision because you are being more careful. Stop and think about what your emotions are telling you. Maybe you're not sure what to do.

Sometimes, people have trouble coming up with good options. Or they might need help making decisions. Keep in mind that you can always talk to an adult you trust if you are having difficulty making decisions. They can provide a new **perspective**.

Sometimes, you may feel confused or overwhelmed when making a decision.

Make a Decision

After you have thought about all your options and the outcomes, you are ready to make a choice.

Be flexible! Be open-minded! For example, you might decide to play with your friends instead of playing with your siblings. But maybe you also decide that once you have spent an hour with your friends, you will go home and play with your siblings.

Making a decision can be tricky. You need to pay attention to your feelings. Ask yourself, *What's best for me? What's best for others involved?*

Sometimes, making a decision can be difficult. It can make you feel worried. Many times, people are scared to make decisions. Don't be afraid to ask for help if you need to. Think about all your options, and pick the best one. Try to choose the option that is best and healthiest for everyone involved. Making good choices takes a lot of practice.

Think and Talk

Have you ever asked for help with a decision? What was the outcome?

Brain Energy

Decision-making is a mental process. But did you know it takes physical energy, too? The average adult brain uses 20% of the body's energy.

Making Good Choices

At some point, everyone worries about making a decision. But there are a lot of things we can do to help us make good choices.

Making decisions takes a lot of energy. Did you know your brain needs energy to make good decisions? Eating healthy foods, such as fresh fruits and vegetables, will help fuel your brain. This will help you make good decisions.

Being tired can lead to bad choices. Not getting enough sleep can affect your thinking. It makes it harder to focus. It makes it more difficult to remember things. Getting enough sleep is important. It will help you make good choices.

Staying healthy is key to making good decisions.

Exercise also helps the brain work better. Activities such as running or swimming increase your heart rate. This increases the blood flow to the brain, making it easier for you to make smart decisions.

Eating healthy foods, exercising regularly, and getting good rest will help you think more clearly and make good decisions.

It's recommended that children and young adults get one hour of exercise every day.

Brain Food

Eating blueberries is good for your brain. They can help improve memory. Other foods that are good for your brain include oily fish, broccoli, and dark chocolate.

Reflect on the Outcome

After you've made your choice, you should reflect on the results of your decision. Did it have a positive or negative outcome? This is the last step in the decision-making process.

Ask yourself, *Did my decision solve the issue? Am I happy with my choice?*

If you make a choice that you end up not feeling happy about, don't feel bad. Everyone makes mistakes. And it's important to learn from our mistakes. This is one way we learn **valuable** lessons.

What if you decided not to tell anyone you were going to a friend's house after school? As a result, you got into trouble because your family was worried about where you were. This is a valuable lesson. Next time, make sure to tell someone where you are going.

Remember to trust your feelings and knowledge. Don't be afraid to ask for help! If you're not happy with your decision, you might need to try a different option next time.

Colors and Mood

Colors can make a difference in your mood. Blue is a calming color. Red and yellow together can make you hungry.

After you've made a decision, you can reflect on it with other people.

Responsible Decisions

Think of all the choices you make every day. Decisions can be challenging. Some of your choices will make a big difference in your life. Some of your choices can affect other people.

Healthy decision-making is an important skill that involves many steps. Next time you need to make a decision, just remember the six steps:

1. **Identify your question**—Know exactly what you are trying to decide.

2. **Gather information**—Keep in mind your values.

3. **Brainstorm options**—Make a list of all the possibilities.

4. **Consider the consequences**—Think about both good and bad outcomes.

5. **Make a decision**—Choose the best option for everyone involved.

6. **Reflect on the outcome**—Analyze your decision.

Step 6 Reflect on the outcome

Step 5 Make a decision

Step 4 Consider the consequences

Step 3 Brainstorm options

Step 2 Gather information

Step 1 Identify your question

It can take time and thought to make a responsible decision. It's up to you to make good choices!

Glossary

amygdala—the part of the brain that is responsible for emotions, such as fear

aware—having knowledge about

complexity—the quality or state of being difficult to understand

emotions—strong feelings (such as anger, love, joy, or fear) that are sometimes accompanied by physical reactions

experience—the knowledge or skills that come from having done or gone through something before

flexible—able to change

impact—a powerful effect something has on a person or situation

knowledge—the range of a person's understanding and information they have learned

lobe—a rounded part

options—things that can be chosen from

outcomes—situations that occur as results or consequences

perspective—point of view; an accurate rating of what is important and what isn't

survival—continuation of living

triggers—causes or brings about, especially a type of reaction

valuable—of great worth

Index

amygdala, 10–11

bad choices, 24

brain, 10–11, 23–25

brainstorm(ing), 16–18

consequences, 18, 28–29

danger, 11

energy, 23–24

exercise, 25

fear, 11

feelings, 18, 20–22, 26

gather information, 14, 16, 28–29

good choices, 22, 24, 29

healthy foods, 24–25

heart rate, 25

mistakes, 26

positive outcome, 18

prefrontal cortex, 10

six steps, 12, 28

sleep, 12, 24

survival skills, 11

valuable lessons, 26

values, 14–15, 28

Civics in Action

It is important to become an active and engaged member of a community. One way to do this is to make good decisions. Or you can help other people make them. Sometimes, it is helpful to talk through issues. Good community members will support one another. Together, they make the right decisions.

1. Read about a decision someone is trying to make. For example, maybe your governor is trying to figure out how to spend state money.

2. Think about the steps to making decisions. Write ideas for each step. Decide what you think is best.

3. Write a letter or email to this person.

4. Give your opinion as to which decision they should make. Explain the steps you went through to help you make your decision.